W9-APJ-389

RADSPORTS GUIDES

MOUNTAIN BIKING

TRACY NELSON MAURER

796.6
MAU

Rourke
Publishing LLC
Vero Beach, Florida 32964

Kennedy Library
77th and Central Ave
Burbank, IL 60459

© 2003 Rourke Publishing LLC

All rights reserved. No part of this book may be reproduced or utilized in any form or by any means, electronic or mechanical including photocopying, recording or by any information storage and retrieval system without permission in writing from the publisher.

www.rourkepublishing.com

Project Assistance:
Chris White and his team at Ski Hut in Duluth, MN, contributed expertise, enthusiasm, and attitude. (Again!)

Also, the author extends appreciation to the Ramos family, Sierra-at-Tahoe Resort, Mike Maurer, and Kendall and Lois M. Nelson.

Photo Credits:
Cover: © Allsport; pages 4, 31, and 39: © Brian Bahr/Allsport; page 7: © Tony Duffy/Allsport; pages 8, 15, and 29: © Eyewire; page 10 and 43: © Mike Powell/Allsport; page 11: © Nathan Bilow/Allsport; pages 14 and 16: courtesy of K-2 Bikes; pages 19 and 20: © CSL; page 44: courtesy of Amber Ramos

Cover photo: Mountain bike racing tests riders' skill, strength, and courage. Even the bravest riders always wear helmets, pads, gloves, and other safety gear.

Editor: Frank Sloan

Cover and page design: Nicola Stratford

Notice: This book contains information that is true, complete and accurate to the best of our knowledge. However, the author and Rourke Publishing LLC offer all recommendations and suggestions without any guarantees and disclaim all liability incurred in connection with the use of this information.

Safety first! Activities appearing or described in this publication may be dangerous. Always wear safety gear. Even with complete safety gear, risk of injury still exists.

Library of Congress Cataloging-in-Publication Data

Maurer, Tracy, 1965-
   Mountain biking / Tracy Nelson Maurer.
      p. cm. — (Radsports guides)
Summary: Surveys the history, equipment, techniques, safety factors, and competitions in the sport of mountain bike riding.
   ISBN 1-58952-277-X
   1. All terrain cycling—Juvenile literature. [1. All terrain cycling.] I. Title.
   GV1056 .M39 2002
   796.6'3—dc21
                                          2002008187

Printed in the USA

CG/CG

TABLE OF CONTENTS

Mountain bike riders do the wild things that couch potatoes talk about doing.

HIT THE DIRT

Most people avoid mud puddles, speeding down rocky slopes, and jumping off boulders (with or without bikes). In fact, most people sit on their duffs, talking about the crazy things other people do.

Mountain bike riders are not like most people. They happily rip through mud puddles. They hunt for off-road trails, especially trails with steep hills, and they steer clear of pansy-smooth paved bikeways.

Mountain bikers usually come home after a ride with layers of dirt, a few bruises and scratches, maybe broken bike parts, and, sometimes, broken body parts. Riders fear one thing: talking instead of doing.

chapter
ONE

DOWN THE MOUNT

Italy takes credit for building the first bikes with rear **suspension** to absorb impact. Italian soldiers used these early cross-country bikes during World War I. By 1930, a few California riders adapted the design.

Forty years later, the off-road biking idea finally gained speed—a lot of speed. Gary Fisher, Joe Breeze, Charlie Cunningham, and other brave riders trucked their bikes up Mount Tamalpais near San Francisco. Then they blasted down the fire roads, sparking an entirely new kind of bike riding.

FAT TIRES FIRE UP

Early riders smoked their coaster brakes on those huge downhill runs. So, they tried motorcycle brake levers. Other tweaks followed. They experimented with fat and knobby tires, angled tube designs, and space-age materials. They added gears after grunting up the mountain a few times. Bikes became lighter, stronger, and easier to control.

By the 1980s, mountain biking grew from a California fad to a worldwide sport. Mountain biking became an official Olympic event at the 1996 Games in Atlanta. Today, millions of mountain bikers tackle rough terrain on safari in Africa, in the outback in Australia, up and down the Swiss Alps, and from coast to coast across North America.

Today, riders as young as 7 years old race their bikes down mountains.

Riding mountain bikes has become a great way for families to enjoy the outdoors.

SUNDAY RIDERS

Mountain bikes (MTBs) make handy transportation for kids. Many adults also commute to and from work on mountain bikes. Riders use their mountain bikes for touring, exercising, and taking Sunday family cruises, too.

HELLO, SPEED FREAKS

Mountain biking also branched into several kinds of competitions. The International Cycling Union **sanctions** the professional World Cup events held in the U.S. and Europe each year. **Amateur** speed freaks enter contests all over the world, too.

Cross-country races attract the most riders of all MTB competitions. Cross-country events look like motocross races with hairpin turns, jumps, and other rugged terrain. MTB races may use laps to cover a certain distance in about two hours. Others might last for a set time, such as brutal 24-hour marathons. Enduros, like motocross endurance races, test the riders' bikes and bodies for several days.

RAD TRIVIA

Collect Schwag
Racers collect freebies, or schwag, from cycling events, exhibitions, and demonstrations. You can also find these stickers, water bottles, and other promo items on the manufacturer and bike magazine Web sites—if you're willing to share your e-mail info.

SUMMER ON THE SLOPES

MTB races borrowed racing ideas from motocross and from skiing. Dual slalom events, like downhill skiing, pit two racers at a time on a short course. Sharp technical skills shave fractions of seconds off the winner's time. The loser sits in the chalet. Skiing inspired MTB races on snow, too. (Now, that's extreme.)

Downhill ski slopes also host many of the downhill MTB races. Riders often top 50 miles (80.5 km) per hour ripping down the course. Races last just a few minutes, when they're pokey.

CHILLIN' WITH CYCLO-CROSS

If you're not up for riding ski slopes in the winter, you might want to try cyclo-cross. This off-season workout has become its own sport.

In the 1920s, European riders blended road-riding and running for winter training. They often carried their bikes over their shoulders as they ran. The idea geared up in the 1990s as MTBs became lighter and riders wanted more full-season excitement.

Now special one- or two-mile (1.6- or 3.2- km) loop courses use **obstacles** and barriers to make riders jump off their rigs and run with them. A race takes 30 to 60 minutes. The SuperCup reigns as the ultimate Cyclo-Cross race, but most events take a less formal, and more friendly, attitude.

Lighter weight bikes have made cyclo-cross even more popular.

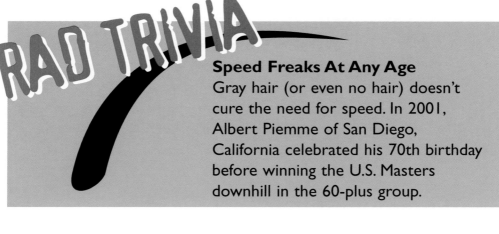

RAD TRIVIA

Speed Freaks At Any Age
Gray hair (or even no hair) doesn't cure the need for speed. In 2001, Albert Piemme of San Diego, California celebrated his 70th birthday before winning the U.S. Masters downhill in the 60-plus group.

FREERIDING TAKES OFF

Organized races stoke some podium-climbing riders. Other MTB riders can't stand the rules and fierce competition. These adventurers turn back toward the sport's thrill-riding roots. They ditch the stopwatches, medals, and prizes for a pure, natural rush instead.

They find their playgrounds far from the groomed trails. You might want to play here, too, but no newbies and no cry-babies allowed.

You need strong technical skills, physical fitness, and steady nerves to conquer the snakes (one-wheel-wide beams or log bridges), boulder ramps, ladder whoops (bumps and bridges), drops, and other gnarly snarls.

You also need the right bike. Cross-country bikes are too light. But, too much weight drags your power on the uphill grinds. **Back-country** bikes use disc brakes, reinforced frames, and rear suspension.

Freeriding isn't about the prettiest bike. It's about the bike that's still in one piece with the rider still on board at the end of the session.

RAD TRIVIA

Park Paradise
A few modern cities see MTB riding as a way for kids to unplug and burn energy. Port Moody in British Columbia opened a City Trials/Stunt Park in its downtown area, thanks to partnerships with local organizations, parents, and kids. Skate parks broke the barrier first. MTB parks could be next. Pitch in to build yours.

YOUR VERY OWN MTB

Back in the 1980s, mountain bikes were *mountain* bikes. You rode them up the mountain so you could ride them down the mountain. If you hit some rough terrain along the way, that made the ride even better.

Today's MTBs look alike at first glance. They all have fat, knobby tires, several gears, and heavy-duty tubing to handle a beating on the trail without falling apart. But different bike designs work better for certain styles of riding. Each bike design balances speed, comfort, and performance with strength. Your skill level and bank account also affect your decision.

chapter
TWO

BIKE BUYERS: BEWARE

Your local Big-Mart sells mountain bikes that look good for about $100. If you don't ride hard and you just want to look good, then you'll find a lovely bike there.

If you really want to ride a mountain bike, then buy a *real* mountain bike. Good used bikes are rare. Riders save their beater bikes for parts. You might find deals on the Internet and in mail-order catalogs. Service and support lags there, however.

Your best bet? Save up the money—around $600 or more. Then spend time in the local cycle shop. The staff there usually knows a lot about bikes and gear. Ask the shop salespeople questions. Follow their advice. Check with them about tune-ups and maintenance, too. (You might pull in some schwag, too!)

FIT YOUR FRAME

The staff should fit the frame to your body. Stand over the top tube with your feet flat on the ground. The saddle, or seat, should touch your lower back. Lift up the front wheel until the top tube touches your crotch. The wheel should be about 3 to 5 inches (7 to 13 cm) off the ground.

Your riding style should also match the frame. Racers like a longer top tube. Freeriders might prefer a shorter sprocket-to-sprocket distance for better control.

3 to 5 inches
(7 to 13 cm)

Stand over the bike and pull the front off of the ground.

You should be able to stop your bike and comfortably straddle the top tube.

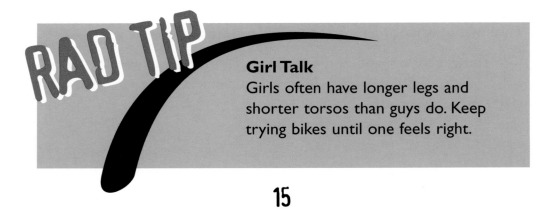

RAD TIP

Girl Talk
Girls often have longer legs and shorter torsos than guys do. Keep trying bikes until one feels right.

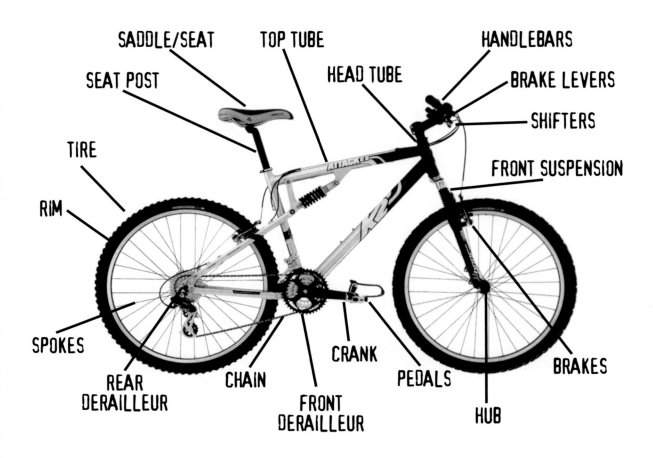

SADDLE/SEAT TOP TUBE HANDLEBARS

SEAT POST HEAD TUBE BRAKE LEVERS

SHIFTERS

TIRE FRONT SUSPENSION

RIM

SPOKES

BRAKES

REAR
DERAILLEUR CHAIN CRANK PEDALS

FRONT
DERAILLEUR HUB

FRAME MATERIALS

Most starter MTB frames use carbon-steel tubing. It's strong and absorbs shock. If you're handy, you can fix it. Manufacturers fine-tune frame construction all the time. Aluminum **alloys** might be the answer one year. Carbon fiber or Kevlar **composites** might be the hit the next year. You'll also see high-end titanium alloys or combinations of these materials, too.

Materials, tube shape, and tube size affect the bike's weight, rust-resistance, strength, and cost. Before you plunk down your cash, know what you really need.

KNOW YOUR TRANNY

Like a car, your bike has a transmission. The crank transmits your energy into movement. It drives the chainrings that use metal teeth to pull the chain in a loop. The chain turns the cassette, or toothed rear hub sprocket, and the rear wheel spins forward.

Gears maximize your energy. Use the shifters on the handlebar to change gears. One shifts down to spin the wheels faster and easier on uphill climbs. The other gear shifts up, spinning the wheels slower and harder for long strides on the flats. Indexed gears click once for each gear.

The **derailleurs** (a French word for *redirect*) change the gears and slip the chain to the proper chainring. MTBs use from 21 to 27 gears.

DRIVE WITH YOUR FEET

Speed plus strength equals power. Your feet power the pedals. Strap your feet to the pedals to improve your power. Toe clips look like metal cages for your feet. Other pedal systems use clipless designs that work with special cleats on your shoes. Some downhill racers and advanced freeriders use no clips at all. They want their feet free to touch the ground for extra balance on corners and jumps.

Match the suspension to your riding style, too. Generally, your front or rear suspension should travel, or move up and down, any where from 3 inches (75 mm) to over 4 inches (100 mm). Racers prefer less suspension to focus their energy on speed. Freeriders want the heavy-duty shock absorbers.

WHEEL WISE

Manufacturers balance weight and strength in their wheel designs. For most MTB riders, strength is critical. Most bikes use 26 inch (70 cm) wheels with alloy rims and 28, 32, or 36 spokes. Match your tire treads, with or without inner tubes, to the terrain you face most often. Serious riders own at least two sets of tires.

While you're checking out your wheels, look for a gizmo called a freewheel on the rear hub. The freewheel uses ratchets and springs to let your wheel spin forward, even if you stop pedaling or pedal backward. It's the gadget that helped make coaster brakes old news.

STOP RIGHT THERE

Some of today's MTBs use disc brakes like a car. Most use V-brakes that pinch the wheel to stop. Some entry-level bikes and many older MTBs use **cantilever** brakes that look more like a U than a V.

Mount the brake levers on the handlebar so that your middle fingers can pull them without lifting your hands off the grips. Your wrists should stay straight, too. Put the rear brake on the right handlebar. Put the front brake on the left handlebar.

RAD TIP

The Brake Hand
You'll use your right, or rear, brake most often. Front brakes stop your bike better than back brakes. Watch out! If you jam the front brakes on a fast, sharp downhill run, you'll endo, or go end-over-end. Feather your brakes for more control.

Mountain bikes are known for their fat tires with deep treads.

The chain and gear system should be kept clean of dirt and well lubricated.

Clean your bike after every session. Use a garden hose to gently spray off mud. Never use a pressure washer!

BIKE BATHS

Your bike works better when you treat it right. Read the owner's manual. Make a maintenance check-list and tape it to your garage wall.

After every session, hose the mud off your bike. Clean your bike with mild soap. Cheap dishwashing liquid works fine. A sponge and paintbrushes reach the bike's odd angles. Look for any cracks in the tubes as you dry the rig. Take the wheels off and clean them, too.

LUBE JOBS

A citrus-based **degreaser** on the sprockets, chainrings, chain, and rear derailleur pulley wheels removes the grease and oil. Clean the parts and use a **paraffin**-based bike lubricant from your local shop to keep your drive train clean. Squeeze a drop of chain lubricant on each link. Wipe the brake surfaces after your lube job.

Bring your bike to a bike shop for regular tune-ups and service. Professional repairs cost a few bucks, but they're cheaper than some of the damage you can do "fixing" major problems on your bike at home.

FIXER UPPERS

Serious MTB riding dings up your bike. Freeriding trashes a lot of parts, too. Maintain your rig and learn to handle the *minor* problems. Buy a bike stand and good tools, including a spoke wrench, cable cutters, and other bike-specific tools. Ask your local bike shop for ideas, too.

While you're shopping for tools, pick up extra chain lubricant, at least one spare chain, a foot pump, and a tire gauge. MTB tire valves aren't always the standard car-tire valves. You may need to add a "presta" valve adapter on your shopping list, too.

MISSION-CRITICAL GEAR

If you ride a bike—any kind of bike, wear a helmet. If you downhill race or freeride, wear a full-face helmet. Approved helmets are required for most races or big rides. Shatter-proof sunglasses or goggles guard your eyes from glare, wind, grit, insects, branches, and other blinding forces. If you wear glasses to see, try prescription lenses or ask about safety lenses.

Downhillers and freeriders also wear motocross-style **armor** on their chests, arms, and legs. The lightweight plastic cushions your body during a crash. It also helps shield you from painful scrapes, punctures, or other injuries.

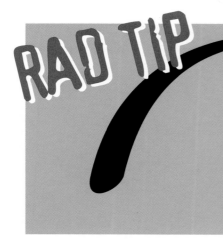

Pump It Up
A gas station air hose can easily explode a bike inner tube with an amazing BANG. A foot pump helps you put in just the right pounds per square inch, or psi. Look on the tire sidewalls for the proper psi for your tires.

HELMET WITH
FACE GUARD

GOGGLES

FACE GUARD

ELBOW PADS

PADDED GLOVES

KNEE AND SHIN
GUARDS

MTB SHOES

23

WHAT ELSE CAN YOU BUY?

Money disappears quickly in a bike shop. What gear should you purchase?

Gloves

Many bikers use gloves to prevent blisters and add gripping power. Gloves also avoid road rash, or cuts and scrapes, in a crash.

Shoes

You might want snug-fitting MTB shoes. (Don't forget to put the pedal clips on the soles, if you upgrade your pedals to a step-in system.)

Padding

Padded bike shorts keep your rear end and other private parts from screaming during a long ride. Even baggy freerider shorts use padded seat inserts. Don't wear underwear with bike shorts. Girls: buy *women's* padded shorts. The padding in men's shorts pinches in bad places. Wear a sturdy sports bra, too. Guys: wear protection, especially if you're freeriding. Make sure your saddle is **anatomically** correct for a girl or a guy.

Comfortable Clothes

Plan to dress in layers. Mountain weather can change quickly. Avoid cotton. A breathable jersey with pockets works well. Pack a warm, quick-dry jacket and a rain jacket, too.

RAD TIP

Drink Up

You sweat a lot riding a bike. Replace fluids by drinking plenty of water. Drink a full liter at least 20 minutes before your session. Drink more water every 20 minutes. If you want to buy something cool, try a hands-free water system, like the Camelbak brand. You can drink on the go and avoid sips from a mud-caked nozzle.

READY TO ROLL

You're geared up and ready to roll. But where? Find an empty parking lot to try out your gears and brakes. Then plan a trip. Keep your first ride under 10 miles (16 km). Practice taking mental notes of landmarks, in case you get lost. Experiment with different gears as you explore new terrain.

Call your state's Department of Natural Resources for help finding open mountain biking trails. Talk to the local bike shop staff about trails suited to your skill level. Ask about MTB clubs in your area, too. Group rides help you improve your skills quickly and show you many different trails. You might meet a riding buddy there, too.

chapter
THREE

THE TRAIL MIX

Many city, state, and national parks maintain trails for visitors. Guests include bikers, hikers, horseback riders, and other non-motorized sports fans. The mix steams up when bikers charge past horses or splash mud on hikers. Reckless riding chokes the fun factor. It also closes trails.

The International Mountain Bicycling Association (IMBA) and other MTB organizations focus on stopping rude riders and fighting trail closings. Help them out. Ride nice. Stay on marked trails. Don't ride in mud and stay off wet trails. Leave nothing but your tire tracks behind. Even better, pitch in on trail workdays.

MTB Safe Riding Rules
- Wear a helmet. Always.
- Ride with a buddy.
- Tell an adult where you're going and when you'll return.
- Stay on open trails only.
- Control your bike speed.
- Yield the trail to walkers, hikers, horseback riders, and other trail users.
- Pass carefully, announcing which side you plan to pass on.
- Check the weather forecast before you go and bring a map.
- Complete a pre-ride check.
- Respect nature. Leave wild animals and plants alone, and don't litter.

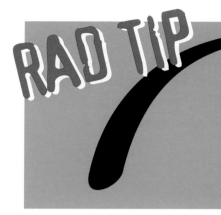

RAD TIP

Don't Go Wild
Steer clear of wild animals. Moose, elk, bears, alligators, snakes, and other dangerous critters usually run away from bikes. Usually. Don't push your luck. Check with park rangers or patrol officers for any special alerts, too.

PUMPED FOR POWER

Pumping pedals pumps your heart and other muscles. During a one-hour ride, each knee bends about 5,000 times. Warm up for about ten minutes before your session turns serious. Never stretch cold muscles.

At the end of the session, cool down with slow riding and stretch for another ten minutes. Stretch your neck, arms, torso, and legs—you use nearly every muscle group riding a MTB! Hold each stretch for 60 seconds.

Kennedy Library
77th and Central Ave.
Burbank, IL 60459

OFF-BIKE DAYS

Use your off-days and off-season to build strength. Push-ups, sit-ups, and weightlifting improve your control, balance, and **flexibility**. You lower your risk of injury, too. Eat right and rest, too. Sleep keeps your mind sharp and helps your body heal for the next session.

Cross-Training Choices
Try motocross, in-line skating, or indoor spinning workouts for cross-training results. Some serious riders also use a trampoline to build flexibility and try ideas for tricks.

Like runners, bike riders should stretch their muscles to prevent injury. This quad, or thigh, stretch works well for MTB riders.

SADDLE UP

Before you start your session, check all the quick releases and tire pressure. Double-check the saddle height. With your feet flat on the ground, the top tube should be at least 4 inches (10 cm) below your crotch. Hop onto the saddle and pedal slowly, watching your knees. When you push the pedal all the way down, your knee should bend slightly. When your pedal comes up, the knee should bend no more than a 90-degree corner.

Cruisers, racers, and freeriders use different **stances**, or positions. Stretching forward to load the front wheel helps cross-country riders build force on the pedals. Freeriders use a more centered stance, shifting weight forward and backward to balance through rough terrain.

STAY LOOSE

Always keep your elbows and knees slightly bent and loose. These joints help absorb impact as you rumble over rough terrain. A tense or hunched body takes a pounding. You wear out faster and lose your control.

Grip the handlebar firmly, but without locking down hard. Keep your wrists in line with your forearms. Your fingertips should easily reach the levers. Thumbs stay on the grips, not on top of the bar.

UUUHHHP HILL

Nothing makes climbing uphill easy. A few things make it less painful, like shifting into a lower gear. Move your weight back on the saddle just enough to gain traction—too much and you risk an ugly backflip. Try lowering into a crouch and pulling the handlebars with your elbows level with the grips. Pick a line, or route, through the terrain and stay on it. Turning loses momentum and traction.

A straight route up a hill keeps your momentum steady.

RAD TRIVIA

Pedal Power
Draw ovals with your big toes or your ankles to spin the pedals. Hammering the pedals up and down wastes energy. For more power, dig your heels down and point the toes up on each push.

DOWN HILLLLLL

You earned your ride down. But share the rush with a buddy. A crash could huck you over the side of the mountain in a flash. Of course, wear your helmet and cover any skin you want to keep.

As you start down, shift your weight back and stretch out your arms. Falling off the back is less painful than a handlebar nosedive.

Check your speed, especially on switchbacks—those hairpin turns that snake down the mountainside. Try not to brake while you turn. Also, don't drag the brakes. Steady braking smokes the rims and heat-glazes the pads. Feather the brakes, avoiding the front brake.

Relax and enjoy the ride.

Feather your brakes on the way down. Dragging them damages the rims and pads.

Stay alert for logs and rocks on the trail. Launching over the front of your bike is not a healthy way to wipe out.

DROPPING IN ISN'T DROPPING OFF

Drops, sharp terrain dips, test your skills.

Dropping in, or copying, means you follow a line over the edge with your front wheel. Shift your weight back until the rear wheel clears the edge. Don't use the front brake. Shift your weight forward once you start to level off.

Dropping off, taking a wheelie into the dip, shows your control and style. Just as you roll the front tire over the edge, shift your weight back and pull up on the front wheel. When the rear wheel drops off the edge, stand on the pedals and move your weight forward for balance. The rear wheel touches down first. Bend your arms and legs for the impact. Ride on.

GOAT HEADS AND OTHER OBSTACLES

Stay alert. Rocky outcrops, called goat heads, logs, **ravines**, sand, water, mud, and other obstacles demand your full attention. Scan the trail about 16 feet (5 m) ahead. Look where you want to ride.

When you hit a patch of nasty terrain, avoid slamming the brake. Steady, medium speed often works the best, even in sand. Keep your body loose, use an easy gear, and move your weight backward to add more traction.

BAIL BACKWARD

Even the best MTB riders biff. Bail before you build speed by pushing backward off the bike. Tuck into a ball and let your hips or bottom take the impact. Don't stick out your hands to break your fall. Fighting gravity creates harsh injuries. Roll with it (unless a tree, boulder, or cliff requires that you dig and skid to a stop to save your life).

RAD TIP

Pack Right

Before you go, rub on sunblock, especially on scars. Also spray yourself with insect repellant. Pack lightly but wisely:

- Spare tube, puncture repair kit, proper valve, and pump
- Pocket knife and specialized bike multi-tool
- Whistle and flashlight (rescuers look for six blasts or flashes separated by one-minute pauses)
- Energy bar and water
- Money and personal ID
- Detailed map and compass
- Waterproof windbreaker
- First-aid kit
- A change of clothes for after the ride

BIG ACTION AND BIG AIR

Every session improves your skills. Practice, practice, practice. The racers, stunt riders, and freeriders you see on TV, videos, and ads didn't start riding yesterday. They work hard to dial in their moves. They get hurt, too.

Sometimes tricks come in handy on more difficult trails, especially single-tracks—one-bike paths that leave little room for error. Wheelies, bunny hops, and jumps can help you avoid obstacles. They show your skill and style, too.

chapter
FOUR

FLYING LESSONS

Before you learn tricks, dial in your balance and control. Landing any trick depends on how well you shift your weight to position your body and bike. Timing and luck help, too. Wear a helmet—no excuses. Always start on easy terrain. And have fun!

RADTRICK: WHEELIES
Risk Factor: 2 out of 10

Wheelies let you pop over roots, logs, stones, ravines, or drops. Start with medium speed in a medium gear. Load your weight on the handlebar with your arms. Ready? Kick down hard on the pedal as you quickly shift your weight back and pull up on the handlebar. Adjust your weight to balance. The very best professional riders can ride one-handed (after a lot of practice and many painful wipeouts).

RADTRICK: BUNNY HOP
Risk Factor: 2 out of 10

Bunny hops let you bounce up and over obstacles. Your legs and arms become your springs, launching the bike as much as 3 feet (1 m) off the ground—with lots of practice.

Start at a medium speed with the bike in a medium gear. Bend your arms and load your weight onto the front wheel. Crouch low with

38

Big air tricks are rare on MTBs. The best riders practice and wipe out a lot before they can pull tricks.

your knees bent. About 3 feet (1 m) before the obstacle, launch your legs like springs popping out and pull up hard on the handlebar. Yank your stomach muscles to help lift the bike, too. Land with your weight slightly back, knees bent, and the rear wheel touching the dirt first.

RADTRICK: JUMPS

Risk Factor: 6 out of 10

Use your skill and control to turn bumps, gullies, drops, and even rocks into ramps. Look far ahead and scout your landing zone on big-air jumps. Blind landings break bikes and bones, or worse.

Keep your knees and elbows bent. Hit the base of the ramp crouched with your weight forward on the handlebar. Stand up slightly as you run up the ramp and let the bike push toward your body. At the lip, or top of the jump, shift your weight back and pull up with your abs for lift. Adjust your weight to keep the bike balanced. Then push the bike away, stretching out your arms and legs. Guide the rear wheel down first. Stomp the landing and ride it out!

RADTRICK: TABLETOP

Risk Factor: 10 out of 10

Dial in your jumps first. Find a jump that gives you decent hang time, at least three seconds of air. Aim for at least 2 feet (.61 m) of **amplitude** or height off the lip. Speed helps. Practice moving the bike around in flight a few times.

For a sick tabletop, use your abs to lift the bike up high just as you pop off the lip. Twist at the waist, tipping the bike to one side with your feet. Push on the handlebar to control the level. You probably won't flatten the bike on your first try. (Plan to eat a lot of dirt practicing this!) A 45-degree angle is a good start. Practice until you can hit a full 90 degrees. Shift your weight back as you crank the bike into its upright landing position. Take the rear wheels down first.

OVER THE EDGE

Mountain bike riding exploded onto the sports scene in the last twenty years. EXPN and other "extreme" sports broadcasts showed the world just how far MTB riders push their skills now. Snow mountain bike racing at the Winter X Games left audiences cheering for more wild MTB action.

Like other extreme sports, MTB now has sponsors, judges, contracts, rules, and other hoo-haw. A few new-school riders ignore the hype and stick to ripping the toughest back-country single-tracks they can find.

chapter
FIVE

PROFESSIONAL RIDERS

Most professional MTB riders compete in cross-country and downhill events. France and Italy really support their racers, and the crowds there know the bikers' names like fans in America know football players. MTB riding isn't that big here. Yet.

A few sponsors pay freeriding teams to advertise for them. Kona Factory Clump Big Air riders show off Kona bikes as they fly through the air. One group called the Flow Riders uses portable ramps, snakes, and other hand-made single-tracks to put on freeriding shows. The Flow Riders also maintain some of the most awesome, hard-core woodland single-tracks in the Pacific Northwest—or anywhere in the world.

COMPETITION READY

Many local bike shops and regional clubs sponsor races. Wisconsin hosts one of the largest state races in the country. The Chequamegon (say: sha-WAH-me-gon) Fat Tire Festival runs every September and draws some of the nation's top competitors to its 40 miles (64 km) of grueling woodland trail. Ask your local bike shop about events in your area.

Use the Internet to find training camps for MTB riding, too. You'll also find MTB travel adventures to some of the world's most exotic locations. Riding new trails dials in your skills as you master various terrain.

The secret to MTB riding? Ride, ride, ride!

Mountain bike racing gains new athletes and new fans every year. Check with your local bike shop for races near you.

CHAMPION MATERIAL

Many awesome athletes ride mountain bikes in cross-country and downhill events. As the sport gains champions, watch for Amber Ramos from California. She's smart, talented, and nice. She also trains hard to race in mountain bike events during the summer and freestyle (mogul) skiing contests in the winter.

Growing up in the mountains, Amber and her older brother Travis practice daily. Amber uses the trails to keep fit. Acceptance as a pro mountain biker at the age of 14, Amber is now focusing on training for mountain biking and skiing in the Olympics. Cheer her on!

FAN FOCUS

Name: Amber Ramos
Birthday: September 5, 1986
Hometown: South Lake Tahoe, California
Height: 5'5" (1.65 m)
Weight: 105 pounds (47.6 kg)
Titles: 2000 Junior National Mountain Bike Champion Women, three-time All-American in Cross-Country Running
Cross-Training: Mogul skiing events and cross-country running
Coach/Trainers: Her dad and brother Travis

FURTHER READING

Extreme Mountain Biking, Universe Publishing. Stefano Martignoni, Luciana Rota. New York. 2000.

Mountain Biking: The essential guide to equipment and techniques. Susanna and Herman Mills. New Holland Publishers Ltd., London. 2000.

WEBSITES TO VISIT

www.imba.com

www.usacycling.org

www.silentsports.net

www.velonews.com

www.mbaction.com

www.mountainbike.com

www.bicyling.com

www.nsmb.com

GLOSSARY

alloys (AL loyz) — materials made of two or more metals

amateur (AM uh choor) — an athlete who competes for fun; he or she receives no pay for winning

amplitude (AM pluh tood) — height off a jump or ramp; big air

anatomically (AN a TOM ih ka lee) — made to fit a certain body structure

armor (AHR mur) — pads and other safety gear

back-country (BAK KUN tree) — natural, wild areas or terrain

cantilever (KAN tuhl EVE ur) — on mountain bikes, the wing-like brakes that look like an upside-down U

composites (kum POZ itz) — materials made from mixing two or more metals or chemicals

degreaser (dee GREEZ ur) — a chemical or solution that removes grease and oil

derailleurs (dee RAY lurz) — a French word for redirect; on bikes, the part that changes the gears and slips the chain to the proper chainring

flexibility (FLEK sah BILL uh tee) — ability to bend and stretch

obstacles (AHB stuh kilz) — things blocking a path; in mountain bike riding, these include rocks, logs, and streams

paraffin (PAR uh fin) — a grease or wax made from crude oil

ravines (ruh VEENZ) — narrow, steep valleys often formed by rushing water

sanctions (SANGK shunz) — approves or checks the rules

stances (STAN sez) — different ways to position the body for control and safety

suspension (suh SPEN shun) — the system of shock absorbers connected to the wheel axles

INDEX

ABOUT THE AUTHOR

Tracy Nelson Maurer specializes in nonfiction and business writing. Her most recently published children's books include the *Radsports I* series, also from Rourke Publishing LLC. She lives with her husband Mike and two children in Superior, Wisconsin.